# A Love Li

MW00649029

Made so easy for you... We've even included a time saving personal letter. So, all you have to do is fill in the blanks then put it in a 5 3/4 by 8 1/2 inch envelope. It can even be a gift for yourself!

More than just a book... More than just a card... It's a gift, card, and book all rolled up in one neat, nifty package. Saving time and giving a gift that shows you care is, in part, what making love with life is all about.

Date _____

Dear _____

| | |
|---|---|
| ____ Self | ____ Friend |
| ____ Mom | ____ Girlfriend |
| ____ Dad | ____ Boyfriend |
| ____ Wife | ____ Co-worker |
| ____ Husband | _____ |

I glanced through this charming book and discovered it has great

| | |
|---|---|
| ____ ideas | ____ stories |
| ____ things to do | ____ all of these |

that will enhance ____my ____ your Making Love With Life quotient

It seemed like the perfect gift to give you for

| | |
|---|---|
| ____ Valentines Day | ____ Christmas |
| ____ Your Birthday | ____ Hanukkah |
| ____ Mothers Day | ____ Engagement gift |
| ____ Fathers Day | ____ Independence Day |

____ Just being you, because you're special

other _____

You deserve more than just

| | |
|---|---|
| ____ a card | ____ a book |

____ this, but it is all I can afford right now

other _____

Enjoy this tasty treat. At least it's not fattening. I remain sincerely yours

| | |
|---|---|
| ____ With Love | ____ Best Wishes |

____ Happy Holidays

other _____


Signed _____

# 222 Ways To
# Make Love With Life

# 222 Ways To
# Make Love With Life

## How To Love, Laugh and
## Live In The Moment

# Ken Vegotsky

AGES Publications
Los Angeles, California, U.S.A. & Toronto, Ontario, Canada

Copyright © 1997 by Ken Vegotsky

The author of this book does not prescribe the use of any technique as a form of treatment nor does he dispense medical advice as a form of treatment, for medical problems without the advice of a physician, either directly or indirectly. The only intent of the author is to offer knowledge of a general nature to help you and your doctor cooperate in a jointly agreed quest for health. In the event you use any of the knowledge in this book for yourself, you are prescribing for yourself, in which case you are exercising your constitutional right, but the author, publisher and speakers bureau assume no responsibility for your actions.

All rights reserved. No part of this book may be reproduced or trans-mitted by any means or in any form, mechanical or electronic, or elec-tronically processed, photographed, recorded in audio form, photo-copied for public or private use nor stored in a retrieval and/or informa-tion storage system, in any form without the prior written permission of the publisher and/or author, except for the inclusion of brief quotations in a review.

Any use of the likeness or name of Ken Vegotsky, or the use of the title of this book for seminars, support groups, workshops, classes, study groups and the like requires the prior written approval of **Key*Point* Guest Speakers**™ and/or **AGES Publications**™ and/or Ken Vegotsky at the address marked below. Any unauthorized use constitutes a violation of federal, state and provincial law.

### THE LOVE LIVING & LIVE LOVING SERIES™
### 222 Ways To Make Love With Life
1-886508-24-0
First printing 1997     10 9 8 7 6 5 4 3 2

Library of Congress Cataloging-in-Publication Data on file at the pub-lisher, Adi, Gaia, Esalen Publications Inc. 8391 Beverly St. #323-ML, Los Angeles, CA 90048 Telephone (519)936-9553
Quantity discounted orders are available for Groups. Please make enquiries to Bulk Sales Department at the above address.
Cover Design and Typesetting by Inside Bestsellers
Manufactured in Canada

**Transactional Reporting Service**
Authorization to photocopy items for internal or personal use, or the internal use of specific clients, is granted by Ken Vegotsky the copyright owner, provided that the appropriate fee is paid directly to Copyright Clearance Center, 222 Rosewood Drive, Danvers MA 01923 USA

**Academic Permission Service**
Prior to photocopying items for educational classroom use, please con-tact the Copyright Clearance Center, Customer Service, 222 Rosewood Drive, Danvers MA 01923, USA (508)750-8400

I dedicate this book to you,
the reader.
You are making a difference,
each and every day.

*I vow each and every day, to share with you the
miracles I have found in this greatest of gifts
called life. My mission is not to change the world
but fine tune it for my children, all children.*

Ken Vegotsky

# ACKNOWLEDGEMENTS

I acknowledge with thanks:

The book reviewers and multitude of media people who made *The Ultimate Power: Lessons From A Near-Death Experience/How to Unlock Your Mind-Body-Soul Potential* a National Bestseller. It is through their support and efforts that you, the reader, have embraced my efforts.

I am forever thankful and grateful to these fine folks who started the ball rolling. Tony, Chris and Charlette of KSON, Deborah Ray and Tom Connolly of the Nationally Syndicated show *Here's To Your Health*, Jana & Ted Bart and Karlin Evins of the show *Beyond Reason* on the Bart Evins Broadcasting Co. Network, Rob Andrus, Greg Lanning and Dr. Joseph Michelli, of the *Wishing You Well Show* on the Business Radio Network, Kim Mason of *The Nightside Show* on 1010 AM, Willa and Bob McLean of *McLean & Company*, Heather Beaumont and Mary Ito of *Eye On Toronto*, CFTO, Anne Shatilla of *Lifestyles*, Life Network and Women's Network, Tony Ricciuto of *The Niagara Falls Review*, Lucy Mekler, Julia Woodford of *Common Ground* & *Vitality Magazines*, Susan Schwartz of *The Gazette*, Casey Korstanje of *The Spectator*, Tess Kalinowski of *The London Free Press*, Len Butcher and Dr. David Saul of *The Tribune*, Claus Schmidt & wife of *Bioforce Inc.*, Rev. Mimi Ronnie, Executive Director of the *International New Thought Alliance*, David Brady producer of *Life After Death* series, Dave Hamblin of *The World Times*, Joanne Tedesco of *The Arizona Networking News*, Andre Escaravage of *The Journal of Alternative Therapies*, Tony Trupiano host of *Your Health Alternatives* WPON 1460 AM, Joe Mazza & Sabastion the Wonderdog of *The Joe Mazza Show* on Talk America, and Elvis, Elliot, Christine, John, Aldrun and Danielle at Z–100, the #1 morning radio show in the Tri-State area.

The support of Mark Victor Hansen, New York Times #1 co-author of the *Chicken Soup for the Soul* series, Brian Tracy author *Maximum Achievement*, Jerry Jenkins of *Small Press Magazine*, Barry Seltzer, Lawyer and author *It Takes 2 Judges to Try a Cow*, Fraser McAllan of *Masterpiece Corporation Speakers and Trainers Bureau*, Dr. J. Siegel, Psychologist, Cavett Robert, Chairman Emeritus of the

*National Speakers Association,* Hennie Bekker, Juno Award Nominee, Pam Sims, M. Ed., Education Consultant and author *Awakening Brilliance,* Richard Fuller, Senior Editor of *Metaphysical Reviews,* Dr. Michael Greenwood, M.B.,B. Chir., Dip. Acup., C.C.F.P., F.R.S.A., co-author *Paradox and Healing,* Dottie Walters, President of *Walters Speakers Bureaus International* and author *Speak & Grow Rich.*

The Learning Annex, Open University, Knowledge Shop, Baywinds and the multitude of public seminar companies who are supporting my efforts. Special thanks to Dave Sersta, for giving me the start in the public seminar business.

Dave, Nancy and Ian Christie, Mark Field, Marilyn and Tom Ross along with a host of others, too numerous to list.

My children, Stephanie and Alan, who brighten my life immeasurably. Mom for being there, you're special. Joni, Robbie, Amanda and Ryan for being the wonderful family they are. Louis Alaimo, the best paver anyone can have do a driveway, but more importantly a great friend, thanks for being there. Sevi for being a friend who is down to earth. Barry Seltzer for being a compasionate lawyer and a great friend. Sheila and Lee, for being authentic.

Mom's incredibly supportive friends: Margo & Colman Levy, Florence & Eli Abranson, Lil Rolbin, Natalie Rosenhek and Sara Shugar. Their souls shine brightly in all they say and do.

Fraser McAllan, a top professional speaking coach. His creativity helped me unleash my Ultimate Power on stage. His company, Masterpiece Corporation Speakers and Trainers Bureau, and Fraser can be reached at (416) 239-6300.

Toastmasters International and the National speakers Association of Tempe Arizona, great people and self-help groups.

Finally, the most important person of all at this time - you! The reader. Your efforts to become a better person by buying this book are the greatest acknowledgment of support I can get. Together we will make this a better world. One person at a time.

Keep on making a difference!

"Make Love With Life"™ became my official trade mark saying at the end of an interview with Dr. Joseph Michelli, psychologist, on his nationally syndicated Business Radio Network show *Wishing You Well.* Life is a gift — a partnership that many take for granted. The following stories, inspirational ideas, sayings, affirmations, humorous and, at times, thought provoking insights are shared with you to enrich your life. May they help you "Make Love With Life" If you do it right, all will be well in your universe.

> *Savor this book. Devour it in one sitting or read one idea, story, action or thought a day. Think of them as vitamins for your well being.*
> *Enjoy!*

# How to access love anywhere — anytime — anyplace

Love is in the air. Stephanie, my daughter, was four years old when she helped me discover this powerful technique. I was leaving for work when she blew me a kiss. Seeing this, I stopped the car... got out... reached up into the air to grasp her homeless kiss in my hand. Then I slapped my cheek, planting her kiss on it. Next I blew her a kiss. She caught on pretty quickly, reaching up, catching my kiss then slapping her face. Then she blew me back another kiss. I caught it and placed it on my cheek. It was a volleyball game of kisses.

Throwing kisses and catching kisses, is one of the safest ways to access the love that surrounds us each and every day.

# Loving thought for today

**"LOVE LIVING AND LIVE LOVING."**

# An "AH–HA!" story...

What is an "AH–HA!" story?

In short, an "AH–HA" story gently demonstrates life enhancing thoughts, ideas or actions. Within each story there are many levels, you may wish to explore. Like a flower blossom which is caressed by the sun until it reveals itself, the "AH–HA!" stories will delicately reveal themselves to you. They will enrich your life and nourish your soul. For fun, see if you discover the nine levels of miraculous messages in this story.

May it give you pleasure, helping you to better Make Love With Life.

Here's one Alan, my son, inspired.

## The Miracles I Have Seen
## HOW TO GROW A BAGEL TREE

Someday I'll write the stories of the big miracles I have seen from the man on the moon and the fall of the Berlin wall to the signing of the Middle East peace accord in the President's garden of roses. Wistfully I say, "Maybe one day I'll write them." Until then, I content myself with the small miracles that abound daily.

I wake up in the morning and this start of the new day is miraculous enough for me. At night I crawl my weary bones and tired body into bed beside that other simple miracle of daily life, my wife of 16 years. That too is wondrous enough for me. You see, it is the simple miracles of daily life that wrap me in wonder. That is what life is about.

Now, take Alan, my 5-year-old pride and joy who is going on 30. He is a miracle that brightens my every day. Last night he did it again!

I had bought some fresh bagels, those round doughy things with a hole in the middle. They were covered in little white sesame seeds that always seem to seek and find the gaps between my teeth. Anyway, here was Alan holding this circle of delightful dough in his tiny hands, happily munching on his bagel. Suddenly, he stopped to ask me, "Daddy, if I plant these seeds, will a bagel tree grow?"

A close friend started to answer him in her typically linear way. I, being the foolish soul I am, took my life in my hands to interrupt her and say, "Alan, if you believe in bagel trees, let's plant the seeds and see."

> *Children have much to teach you and me about discovery, the miracles of life and using our imaginations.*

Well, I don't know about you, but until today I did not believe in bagel trees. Just in case they might exist, Alan and I planted the seeds. You know what? I would not be surprised at all to see bagel trees grow....

In any case, I have proof enough to know that bagel trees really do exist in the imaginations of 5-year-old boys and 41-year-old dads.

Such are the wonders of childhood and parenthood, an awakened sense of discovery and the pleasure of living in the moment. Listen to children. They have much to teach you and me about discovery, the miracles of life and using our imaginations.

An excerpt from<br>
The Ultimate Power<br>
How To Unlock Your Mind-Body-Soul Potential<br>
Ken Vegotsky, AGES Publications

Loving thought for the day

Children are great teachers.<br>
Mine get me to practice<br>
the art of unconditional love,<br>
daily.

# Enrich your life

> Buy a box of passion fruit and share them
> with a friend or partner.

# Point to ponder

> "Our life is frittered away by detail… Simplify, simplify."
>
> Henry David Thoreau

# What is love?

To some, it is a strong affection or liking for someone or something. A passionate affection transcending all other states of being. For others, it refers to the sexual nature of human beings.

# What is life?

Life is a state of being …a state of flow… where people and the physical world share the energy in partnership. One nourishes the other in a cycle that most believe begins with conception and ends in death.

A fuller life is a state of awakened consciousness, a deeper understanding of the very essence of ones being. Each level of awakened consciousness will help you to develop a new focus on life, a directed consciousness about the process of living, and give you the opportunity of rediscovering how to love even the simplest of actions or thoughts. At times, you may laugh which is a wondrous state of being in the moment.

Underlying all this is one of the greatest truths I've come to know. There are only two things you can control — your own thoughts and actions.

Accepting this simple yet empowering idea into your life, allows you to practice free will on a daily basis.

The art of making love with life is minimalist at best, decadent at its worst. In either case you can experience a passion for life and renewed zeal for living.

To life! To love! To all those things which make this journey the most sensual combination of experiences.

> *Two things you can control*
> *– your own thoughts*
> *– your own actions.*
> *Accepting this idea into your life, allows you to practice free will on a daily basis.*

# Why is it...

> When I was younger
> a big heart meant generosity.
> Now I am older,
> a big heart means see the cardiologist.

# The Art of Joyous Non-Attachment

Life's journey is filled with many trials and tribulations, joys and achievements. To enhance your Making Love With Life quotient, a key is to savor each moment without being attached to the outcome. Put another way,

> DO WHAT YOU LOVE AND LOVE WHAT YOU DO.
> THE RESULTS WILL BE WHAT THEY SHOULD BE.

# Roses by the dozen - under a buck!?

Yes. Just follow these instructions. Materials needed paper, scissors and possibly crayons.

1) Buy wrapping paper or Geopaper™ by Geographics with

pictures of long stemmed roses on them. Better yet, draw roses on paper, it's fun.

2) Cut out a dozen red roses. (Remember when you were in school and used to cut paper dolls, snowflakes – come on guys, confess, you also did it, but are suffering a memory lapse.)

> TIP: If you cannot find the specialty paper in your local Staples, The Office Place, Business Depot or stationery supplier, call Geographics head office in Blaine, Washington at (360) 332-6711. Other sources of wonderful specialty paper products are Paper Direct, Secaucus, New York call their toll free number to get a catalog or order (800) 865-8634 and Reliable Corporation, Schaumburg, Illinois call their toll free number to get a catalog or order (800) 735-4000.

# Point to ponder

"The symphony of life is best heard in the silence between its notes. In fact, in a real symphony it is the silences which make the music work best."

> *Unknowingly, we carry many debilitating ideas around with us. Ideas that need to be shed if we are to Make Love With Life.*

# Lucky in love! Lucky in life!

Number 13 is a lucky number, especially for me since you're still reading this book. Especially for you since you got this far and are discovering ideas, stories, thoughts and actions that add value to your life.

So next time you think of number 13 as anything but lucky, put that idea outside the doorway to your mind. Lock it out. Don't let it back inside and get on with Making Love With Life!

# Two of the most important questions you can ask yourself

Have I contributed to humanity?
Have I used my talents and abilities to the maximum?

**E**nrich your life, and that of those around you

**SMILE AT A STRANGER**

**E**rotic and easy dessert – Frozen Grapes

Ingredients: Grapes - as many as you want.
Separate the grapes from the vine. Wash and gently pat them dry. About an hour before you want to eat them, put them in a freezer safe container and pop them into the freezer.

TIP:   Seedless grapes are best for this, but I prefer grapes with seeds. Why? The seeds contain a powerful healing chemical, that is released when you chew on them. The technical name for the active ingredient is 'proanthocanidins'.

Now that is a mouthful!

**P**oint to ponder

"Man is the only animal that blushes… or needs to."
                - Mark Twain

**B**ecome a lazy gardener so you can savor life a little more

How? Convert your lawn from labor intensive to pleasure intensive. Instead of grass plant white clover. Grass needs constant watering, fertilizing and cutting. White clover stays short and needs very little water or cutting. Whereas grass takes more from the soil than it gives back, clover gives nutrients to the soil, such as nitrogen, leaving the soil in better shape. You'll save money, time and energy - which is what making love with life is about.

> TIP:    Farmers supply centers are a great location to get clover. Ask your local garden center to get a supply.

Clover is a flowering plant which attracts bees. In the last decade, the North American honey bee population has been cut in half. In some cases, farmers now have to rent bee hives to pollinate their orchards and crops. Eventually, that means higher food costs, diminishing plant life and poorer air quality. Plant life helps clean the air and gives us oxygen.

# Be a kid again

Get finger paints and paper - now go to it!
or
Do it with a friend and don't use paper as your canvas.
(Some things are better left to one's own imagination.)

# Life renewing trivia of the most important kind

The National Aeronautical Space Administration, NASA, was searching for the best air purifiers they could find. Guess what? They found them all around us.

Plants cleaned the air of toxic gases and fumes, better than any man made contraptions could. They were the most economical air purifiers and the plants throw in a dash of oxygen to top it all off.

> TIP:    Spider plants are the most efficient indoor air cleaners. Ask your local garden supplier for the best plants to use in your area. Your Botanical Garden or library will know which ones purify the air best.

Talking about plants, here's a most loving one that I have discovered.

The Tree of Love
PLANT THE SEEDS TODAY

### Share the love.

This letter of H.O.P.E. (Happiness Of People Expands) and Love is being sent to you, unconditionally. No money is being solicited nor actions required. Unconditional Love starts with acknowledging another – wherever and whomever they are. This is our way of making this a better world - one person at a time.

This Tree of Love was started by Ken Vegotsky, speaker & author of *The Ultimate Power: How to Unlock Your Mind-Body-Soul Potential* and *222 Ways to Make Love With Life* books. The seeds of this branch were sent out by the undersigned asking you to share this message of Unconditional Love so that all may have H.O.P.E. today for a better tomorrow.

To participate in creating more H.O.P.E., make a copy of this letter and give, mail or share its contents with two or more people. Make a difference today. Share the love. Love is the answer! I'm making a difference, you can too. Copy this letter and share your H.O.P.E. and Love with another today!

| My Name is | City | Country | Date |
|---|---|---|---|
| | | | |

This is the North American branch of The Tree of Love. Help it grow into a forest. Feel free to photocopy or hand write The Tree of Love.

Tip: If photo copying, you can more than double its size. Use the 200% or more enlargement feature on the photocopier.

# Enrich your life

Plant a flower – outdoors or indoors.

# The 9 1/2 Laws of Stupidity

Law of Stupidity #1

If you don't know you can't do it - just do it!

Law of Stupidity #9 1/2.

Go back to Law of Stupidity #1

(More of these laws later.)

# Point to ponder

"It takes two to speak the truth, —
one to speak, and another to hear."

Henry David Thoreau

# Being good to your heart and a whole bunch of other body parts, on the cheap. Here's how:

Sprinkle ground up flax seed on salads, sandwich fixings, cereal – be creative. Try to have at least a heaping tablespoon full each day. It is good for kids too. Flax seed, one of the best sources for essential fatty acids which the body needs for optimal functioning, can help your cholesterol level. It has also been known to help restore skin elasticity and help learning disabled children function better. This is a small sampling of flax seeds benefits.

How do you do it?

Buy whole flax seeds, available in health food stores. They are not expensive.

Grind the flax seeds up. A mini food processor or coffee mill works great for this.

Place the ground up flax seeds in a sealed container in your refrigerator. Stored right it stays okay for a very long time.

Now, sprinkle away to your health each day.

# Lovemaking — one of the oldest healing arts

Dr. Mariam Stoppard, author of *The Magic of Sex,* notes the physiological benefits of sexual arousal boost the immune system. In addition, the circulating levels of hormones and endorphins increase. So, people feel better and heal faster.

The benefits to women are quite extensive. A renewed sense of well being and acknowledgement of their inner beauty, in this fashion, is physically, emotionally and spiritually nourishing. After menopause, the increase in testosterone levels, produces a heightened sense of physical need.

> *Love...*
> *has to be made...*
> *remade... made new.*

Interestingly as men age, sexual release can have a positive affect upon enlarged prostrates. This should be of particular interest to men over age 40, the age after which prostrate problems may start occurring. The prostrate is intimately connected with the urological functioning of the male body. A healthy prostrate is important to sexual potency and the ability to urinate. Saw Palmetto and pumpkin seeds are two natural things that help the prostrate function better.

Women's cycles are also enhanced by botanical sources. Evening Primrose oil, which contains an important essential fatty acid, can alleviate the effects of premenstrual syndrome (PMS). This is natures way of making love with humans – by supplying our bodies with life enriching chemistry.

I mention this to make you aware of the subtle, yet essential nature of our fragile existence and partnership with the planet. Honor the earth and it will repay you in kind.

Loving thought for today

> "Love doesn't just sit there like a stone.
> **IT HAS TO BE MADE,**
> like brick: remade all the time, made new."
> Ursula K. LeGuin

Gaia — Greek for Earth Goddess – Its use acknowledges the holistic self-regulating nature of the Earth

Like a mother cares for a child, the planet cares for humanity. The interconnectedness is subtle, dynamic and life enhancing. For example, salt is constantly being feed into the seas by the rivers that feed them. Amazingly these salts remain at a constant level of concentration of three per cent. This self-regulatory nature is essential. If the level of salinity were to double, few sea creatures would survive.

James Lovelock, at a conference in Princeton in 1969, is credited for using this idea of Gaia to expand our perception of the material world. This shift in thought from 'spaceship earth' to Gaia - Mother Earth, is how he showed that even our world Makes Love With Life!

Be a kid again — Reconnect to the earth

Camp out in your backyard with a best friend. Share ghost stories with each other. Wake up in the middle of the night and sneak back into your bed.

# Catching Kisses continued

You're all alone. You need some loving.
Easy!! Catch a homeless kiss.

Step 1   Reach up with an open hand.
Step 2   Grasp a homeless kiss in your hand.
Step 3   Give the kiss a home
            – gently slap it onto your face, now.

If it's a wet kiss, check to see if it's raining. If it is, then savor the feel against your cheek. If it isn't, check to see if someone's watering their lawn.

# Lovemaking 101

Sex expert Sari Locker, author of *Mindblowing Sex In The Real World,* shares these four quick tips:

1) Be in the moment, by taking care of all distracting problems like the phone and protection first.
2) Use the five physical senses – Taste, touch, smell, sight and hearing – when lovemaking.
3) Variety and experimentation are okay.
4) Learn how to pleasure yourself.

ADD this idea to this list.

Find a place where you and your partner can lovingly communicate your wants, needs and desires. Make it a safe place free of distraction or concern for interruption. Listen and share with each other, without passing judgment, as you explore the intimate side of your physical and emotional well being.

# Today, be a kid again

**Go fly a kite.** or
**Howl at the moon.**

Chocolate may not be bad for you!?

Scientists have discovered that chocolate may help release endorphins, thus creating a short lived mildly euphoric state. In moderation, this maybe beneficial to your well being.

>  TIP:   Certain chocolates have lower melting points or come in a spread. With a partner, melted or spread choco- late applied strategically and lovingly, can be quite an all consuming treat.

Energy boosts — required, at times, to Make Love with Life.

Here are five ways to boost your energy levels.

>  1) Use essential oils – peppermint and lemon quickly invig- orate me. I put a drop on a handkerchief/face cloth and inhale their essence. Lemon boosts my feelings of well- ness. The Japanese use it in their office air conditioning systems. It reduced data clerk entry errors a whopping 54%.

>  2) Invest in an air purifier.
>  TIP: I have dozens of the best and cheapest air purifiers on the face of the earth spread throughout my home – plants.
>  Bionaire Corporation of Allendale, New Jersey, produces an excellent HEPA grade, hospital clean air quality standard, home air cleaner. Their toll free consumer information numbers are:
>  U.S.A. (800) 253-2764    Canada (800) 561-6478

>  3) Vitamin deficiencies are a common cause of fatigue. I use a B-complex supple- ment along with iron and magnesium sup- plements when necessary.

*Be kind to yourself by learning what helps you develop the energy needed to invest in life and Make Love With Life*

The B vitamins are water soluble and should be replen- ished daily. Water soluble means that the mechanism your body uses to distribute the nutrient is through liquids, like blood. Excess amounts are removed through urination and sweating.

Iron is particularly beneficial to women, since menstruation causes iron depletion in the body. Good sources of iron are bananas, apricots, sea vegetables, beans and whole-rye grain.

4) Lack of good quality rest and sleep suck the energy from you. Drinking chamomile tea or other specially formulated herbal teas, helps me and my children sleep better.

5) And finally, let there be light. Expose yourself to at least 15 minutes of sunlight a day. Our bodies produce vitamin D this way. If indoors, you may want to use full spectrum lighting. You'll be amazed at the difference in the quality of light.

Health food stores and places like The Home Depot carry these types of lighting.

L oving way to share your fantasies and desires

Book marking is a wonderful way of gently expressing your sexual fantasies and desires. The way it works is simple.

Buy a book of erotic stories – or if you're a little skittish, borrow one from your library. The only problem is that you might feel pressured to return it. If you use the book, that's okay. Just be prepared to pay the fine... Hopefully, a big one.

Splurge, buy a special book mark.

Find a fantasy story that particularly interests you... insert the book mark at that passage... leave the book on your partners night table or hand it to your partner to read at their leisure.

If your partner likes the idea expressed, they return the book with the bookmark in the same place. The two of you reserve a time and... I'll leave the rest up to your imagination.

What does your partner do if they're not interested in the selection? They read more stories... find one that appeals...

insert the book mark to reveal their interest… leave it on your night table.

The main benefit is the gentle way of sharing those seldom discussed needs and wants that often create unnecessary stress – win-win negotiation for the bedroom. Worst is you become a very well read individual. Possibly very very well read!?

> TIP: Joan Elizabeth Lloyd presents this idea, numerous erotic stories for lovers to share and helpful advice in her books, *Come Play With Me, If It Feels Good* and *Nice Couples Do,* published by Warner Books. A wonderful 180 minute audio cassette called *Nice Couples Do* from Time Warner Audiobooks combines parts of the three books in an abridged version. Missing a lot of the stories and detail, the tape is still a great place to start, if you want to explore this aspect to *Make Love With Life.*

# Trivia of the most important kind

Life is a celebration! Lovemaking is a manifestation of this. More than just a physical state, it is an emotional one. Approximately 25% of adults in a survey said lovemaking is the closest they come to connecting to their spiritual side. Is that what is meant by heaven sent?

# It's true!

Chicken soup has curative properties according to a hospital in Florida, which is selling canned homemade chicken soup to raise funds.

You don't have to go to Florida to find incredible chicken soup – it's on the shelves of bookstores throughout the land. Mark Victor Hansen and Jack Canfield are the creators of an inspirational book series called *Chicken Soup for the Soul,* published by Health Communications. This series is a publishing phenomenon, with over 8,000,000 copies sold and more on the way. Three of the books appeared on major bestseller lists – at the same time!

Treat yourself or a friend to a great gift. You'll be inspired and happy you did.

NOTE: This is an unsolicited testimonial for two people who are making a difference. The fact that Mark Victor Hansen gave my first book *The Ultimate Power,* a rave testimonial, has nothing to do with this plug – well maybe a little something.

Thanks Mark and Jack for adding so much sunshine to the lives of millions. They say a great book is passed onto ten others to read. In that case… you do the math to estimate how many people's lives have been enriched and nourished. Acknowledging Jack and Mark, is my way of practicing thankfulness.

I'm looking forward to reading more of the Chicken Soup for the Soul books – especially the upcoming book, which may contain the story I wrote, called *The Blanket.*

Encouraging and empowering others to connect to their higher power is what this series does, plus much more.

What makes this most interesting is that I have never met nor spoken to either of these men. Yet they took the time to help me. Their actions say more than any words can about their character.

> *Dance is a way to unleash the powers of the soul and free one's self from the limitations of the mind's perceptions*

L ose yourself in the moment

Put on comfortable clothing (optional)…
Play wild music…
Dance freely and wildly…
Throw your arms and hands out…
Let your cares and worries fly away…
Spin, twirl and become one with the music and the
song in your heart.

This can be done alone or with others. Many mystical systems use this as a way of reaching ecstasy! At weddings, dancing is the part all may share in tribute to the couple – trying to get the ecstasy ball rolling, so to speak.

Great examples of the power of losing one's self in dance, are the sequences in classic movies such as *Zorba the Greek* and *Fiddler on The Roof.* Rent the videos and see for yourself.

# Acupressure or reflexology for the hurried person

Take a tennis ball and roll it under your bare feet. Did you enjoy it? Yes! Then explore the healing power of a reflexology session with a trained specialist, or find a close friend who will rub your feet.

### *Aaahhh!*

# Enrich your life

Explore the texture of everything you can. Feel the texture of satin garments or sheets. Compare regular to percale woven bed sheets. Discover the sensuality of a silk shirt. Savor the texture of ice cream. Become an explorer of textures.

# The joy of self-loving is expanded upon by Dr. Betty Dodson, a noted sex-therapist.

She created a straightforward and appealing guidebook that reveals satisfying ways to explore your sexual nature. She demonstrates this in a warm and intelligent fashion, suitable for men and women. Self-love is more than just a physical process, it is a way of lovingly affirming your life and human experience.

Interested? Yes. The title of the book is *Sex for One*, by Betty Dodson, Ph.D., published by Crown Trade Paperbacks. Get a copy for yourself, or anyone whom you believe may want to explore this intimate side of themselves.

# Tip to opening minds

Give the man in your life a Harlequin or Silhouette novel. It may help him better appreciate and accept your idea of romance. If he needs some encouragement to read it, bribe him – tell him you'll give him a brief quiz, and if he passes, you'll… I leave that up to your imagination.

Men, give the woman in your life a copy of this book. (Okay I admit it, I'm an unabashed believer in what I write about.) Show her you care.

# The power of thought

Positive self-talk, also known as affirmations, are recordings you can choose to play in your mind. Using them will enhance your life. Repeat this one to yourself, throughout the day.

**"I LOVE MYSELF."**

# Catching Kisses continues

Sometimes I end my speaking presentations demonstrating the art of throwing and catching kisses. I love doing it.

*Practice makes better – Perfect comes from making better better – Repetition is the practice required to better Make Love With Life*

What is most enjoyable is seeing male and female professionals like doctors, managers, bankers, engineers, chiropractors, accountants, etc… dressed in executive attire, throwing and catching kisses. If you ever had hundreds of people throw kisses at you, all at once, you'll realize how fast you have to work to catch as many as you can, before they fly past you.

Amazingly, when I'm catching the kisses the last one always seems to land on my rear cheek. If I ever find out whose aim is so bad, I'm going to give them one big juicy wet kiss – on their face.

The powerful side of catching kisses.

At one convention, a well dressed woman walked up to me to tell me her story.

"Last night, just after your seminar, I drove my 73 year old aunt to the airport. She's been depressed for many months and I couldn't recall the last time I had seen a smile on her face. In the car, I told my aunt you said we could access love anytime and anywhere by catching one of those homeless floating kisses.

My aunt looked at me strangely then smiled for the first time in a very long time. By the time she boarded the plane, she was a totally different person. It was amazing!"

A magical transformation had taken place.

## Enrich your life

Send a love note to a relative you haven't spoken to for awhile.

TIP: You can use the Tree of Love chain letter on page 19.

## FREE LOVE!?!

If romance is your game, buy a copy of *1001 Ways to Be Romantic* by Gregory Godek. If your book store cannot get it, you can order it from this toll free number (800) 432-7444.

Gregory does Romance Seminars and has a fun newsletter full of creative, unusual and wonderful ideas, gifts and gestures, called the LoveLetter. To sign up for the newsletter, write LoveLetter, P.O. Box 226, Weymouth, Massachusetts 02188-0001

Currently, this $25 subscription newsletter is free for the

asking. When you write them, tell them Ken Vegotsky, the speaker and author of *The Ultimate Power* and *222 Ways to Make Love With Life* sent you, and they will waive the subscription cost. Do it soon. This is a time limited offer!

L oving thought for today

>**"AN OUNCE OF LOVE IS WORTH A POUND OF KNOWLEDGE."**
>John Wesley

L oving affirmation for today

>"Love is in the air – it's up to me to catch it."

M ake a note for yourself – fill in the blank with your name

>I _____ Make Love
>With Life each and every day.

Post it on your refrigerator. Recycle a piece of used paper. Making Love With Life means respecting all the ways life manifests itself. Reusing paper is a gentle way to save our forests and our planet.

D iscover a wonderful book

*The Prophet* by Kahlil Gibran, with passages on love, relationships and life in general, will caress your mind, body and soul. Buy extra copies as gifts for your children, your partner or other special people in your life.

Personalize it by writing your comments in the various sections of the book that appeal to you.

I've done this for my children. They're a little young now, but the message I wrote on the cover is that they should read any section dealing with a problem they are having in their life at that time. My comments and his words will guide them to find the answers they need.

The fun part is that you get to write a classic this way, so to speak.

You can choose any book you want that reflects what your ideas on life are about. Have fun searching through your local bookstore.

Catching Kisses... the final frontier!

Give a homeless kiss a home today. With your help, this idea will catch on. Share the idea of catching kisses with a friend or loved one.

TIP: Photocopy the section "How to Access Love anywhere – anytime – anyplace" from on page 11 in this book and post it on your office bulletin board – mail it to a friend in need or better yet, send them a copy of *222 Ways To Make Love With Life.*

Today, create your own loving affirmation

_____
_____
_____
_____

Life affirming loving thought for the day

**"LOVE IS THE APHRODISIAC OF LIFE."**

# Mystery notes

When my children stay with me, or when I'm visiting my mom or a special friend, I leave behind inspirational or thank you notes. I tuck them away in imaginative places... in between a set of plates... in the freezer... inside the pillow case...

By now you've got the idea. My favorite hiding places are on the front of the refrigerator or in the TV Guide.

> *Let the child within you playfully demonstrate*
> *- that you feel the love*
> *- that you respect the love of those around you*

# Aromatherapy — natures gift

Basically, there are four ways to use the essential oils from plants; oral, external, nasal (inhalation) and in cooking.

Read a book by Valerie Woodward, Jo Serrentino or Tisserand. These experts will help you discover how to use oils such as sandalwood, cinnamon and ylang-ylang. Some, you'll discover, may have aphrodisiac qualities.

# Aromatherapy massage — an incredible experience

There are numerous kinds of massages, but my favorite is a Swedish massage combined with the healing or stimulating properties of an aromatherapy essential oil in a good base carrier oil. Treat yourself to a massage and you'll feel like you're in heaven.

> TIP: Budget tight – then call a local school where massage is taught. They need people to practice on. Volunteer – you'll be glad you did!

Health food stores, department stores and The Body Shop may have premixed aromatherapy massage oils.

33

# Love affirmation for today

*"I make love with life."*

# Loving thought for the day

"Hugs are a gentle form of massage."

# Hawaiian Hugs

I created this type of hugging to gently combine touch and a yoga type of breathing to create a connection between two consenting people. It creates synchronicity as the energy flows are gently balanced between two people.

Step 1. Get the main ingredients – two consenting adults.

Step 2. Place your chests against each other, heart to heart.

Step 3. Firmly wrap your arms around each other.

Step 4. Breath in together, through your noses, inhaling deeply. Think of the air you inhale, as coming from heaven.

Step 5. Hold the breath in for a few seconds, then together, slowly release it through your mouths. Think of the exhale as going to the earth. You're blowing out all the junk from your mind and body.

Step 6. Repeat this breathing technique, at least three times before you release your partner.

Step 7. To enhance the affect of living in the moment, close your eyes after a few breaths.

Step 8. Continue hugging.

WARNING: If continued for extended periods, I cannot be held responsible for what happens. Please let me know if the result is a baby boy or baby girl.

# Loving technique to connect to the moment

Whenever you are feeling distracted, try this. Breath slowly and deeply as you say the following to yourself.

**I BREATH IN AND CONNECT TO MY MIND-BODY-SOUL...**

**I BREATH OUT AND SMILE...**

**LIVING IN THE MOMENT... THIS IS THE ONLY MOMENT...**

Keep repeating this until your mind is cleared of chatter. Time your breathing with the thoughts. Continue repeating this saying and focus on your breathing. Feel the life affirming oxygen caressing your lungs. Savor the sensations. Let your worries and distractions melt away with each breath.

Closing your eyes will deepen the relaxation. This works great in times of stress, lovemaking and whenever you want a powerful way to connect to the moment. Trust yourself, the rewards are incredible. Start now, for a few minutes.

This is my expansion of an ancient meditation used first in the Far East to allow the relaxation response to manifest itself.

> *It is often a challenge to realize that many of the difficulties we face is how life makes us aware of the lessons we need to learn*

# Loving affirmation for today

Repeat this frequently throughout the day:

**"I LOVE MYSELF AND ACCEPT OTHERS."**

# Thought provoking insight to help you see life more clearly

**"OUR PERCEPTIONS DISTORT OUR RECEPTION."**

# An "Ah–Ha!" story…

Letting go is an incredibly powerful way to connect to life and the moment. Sometimes you have to mess up your thoughts to succeed. Here's one of my favorite "Ah-Ha" stories:

## A FLIGHT OF FANCY

A traveling salesman decided to relocate to Chicago. He bought a home near enough to Chicago's O'Hare Airport to be only a few minutes drive from it, but far enough away so that the noise from the planes did not bother him.

Many years passed, and O'Hare Airport, one of the world's busiest, put in a new runway. Now, planes flew right over his home. In fact, they flew so close that he could see the passengers' faces peering through the planes' windows. The noise was driving him crazy. His sales starting plummeting, as did his health.

Finally, he sought help from a psychiatrist.

"Either you sell your home and move, or change the way you think about this inconvenience. You don't need me to help you decide what to do," the psychiatrist said, reflecting the salesman's thoughts.

That was the last time the salesman saw the psychiatrist until they bumped into each other a year later.

"So how are you doing?" the psychiatrist asked.

"Great!" replied the salesman. "I'm still in the same house and loving every moment of it."

"What did you do?" the curious psychiatrist asked.

"I painted a sign on the roof of my house with bright white fluorescent paint. The sign says WELCOME TO CLEVELAND."

T rivia of the most important kind

Researchers say the a sneeze has the same force and affect upon the human body as an orgasm.

> P.S.  I don't know about you, but I'd be willing to sign up for a seminar on Sneezing Yourself Into Ecstasy.

A n all natural way to restore your skins youthfulness, and save a bundle.

*Treat Your Face Like A Salad!* by Julia Busch, published by Anti-Aging Press, is a wonderfully delicious book. It uses everything but the kitchen sink to help you inexpensively rejuvenate your skin. It includes natural ways to nourish your skin and body. You'll save a fortune in cosmetics. To order it call toll free (800) SO YOUNG (769-6864)

If her picture on the cover is any indication of the power of her books, I would suggest you use express delivery. She says she is in her fifties, but she looks much younger.

W hy is it...

> When I was a kid, adults looked really old.
> Now that I am older,
> older people look rather young to me.

P ractice Thankfulness — Make a life loving and affirming offer today.

Love offerings can be charitable donations to an environmental group, homeless shelter, home for abused people, animal shelter, church, synagogue, mosque, school, charity or any group that aims to give more than it takes from this universe. Best of all, support those that are trying to save the diversity of life on this planet. Honor this partnership – we are all connected.

Making love with life means realizing that we are all one in partnership with everything in the universe.

Even though the ebb and flow of space and time is beyond our daily awareness, it still affects us. Science proves what poets, artists and writers through the ages have known. I offer you this timeless poem to ponder the power of this idea.

No man is an island, entire of itself;
every man is a piece of the continent, a part of the main;
if a clod be washed away by the sea, Europe is the less,
is well as if a promontory were,
is well as if a manor of thy friends, or of thine own were;
any man's death diminishes me
because I am involved in Mankind;
and therefore never send to know for whom the bells tolls;
it tolls for thee.

John Donne
an English metaphysical poet
who lived from 1573 to 1631.

Treat yourself to the thoughts and words of a very special person. His words resonate reality so naturally. They connect to nature and all things great and small. He enables you to discover his love of life affirming message. His name is Henry David Thoreau. Start with his book *Walden*. Your life will be richer for it.

Henry David Thoreau was an American writer best known for his account of the year he spent alone in the Walden woods in Massachusetts. Another great work he wrote is called Civil Disobedience which laid the cornerstone for non-violent social resistance that Gandhi and others embraced. The sit-ins of the sixties is another example stemming from Thoreaus' ideas. He lived from 1817 to 1862.

> *An abundance of miracles is offered to you each and every day but they are more easily recognized when you Make Love With Life*

T oday make a love offering

Make a donation – to the Walden Pond Preservation Society, Audubon Society, Greenpeace, Save the Dolphins or other group that is trying to protect us from ourselves and the ravages upon the land humanity makes in the name of progress.

T ake an Eco-Tour next time you travel. These are holidays where the travel company makes arrangements to visit parts of the world still in their natural state. They attempt to minimize the impact to our environment and to the native peoples living there. Think of it has being holistic travel, healing and honoring the planet and yourself. Respecting nature is respecting life at the most important level. In turn, nature respects us.

Incidentally, old growth forests in North America are not being replaced in a fashion that sustains our total environment. They are disappearing at an alarming rate. By taking an Eco-Tour, you are supporting the workers who live in the areas, and helping the trees stay alive.

This form of economy can sustain itself indefinitely.

Whereas an ancient tree takes hundreds of years to replace itself, as well as the multitude of creatures that are supported and support the life cycles of the forest.

Log a tree, lose the land. Hug a tree and embrace its life force. Alternatives to logging exist, that would create more jobs and do a lot less damage to our fragile planet.

It is people like you, requesting papers made out of hemp or other grasses that grow rapidly, that can make a critical difference to this planet and the future generations.

P.S. 'Eco' is short for ecological.

A thought provoking insight to help you love life and all it has to offer

*"We are born free, we only chain ourselves."*

S omething you can do, to appreciate life today

Get a glass of water. Raise it to the heavens and make a toast to life. Savor each drop. Water is the wine of life.

So much is taken for granted that even the most common of things is often ignored. Water of all things should be respected.

Put another way – the human body is about seventy per cent water. We need it to survive.

P oint to ponder

**"For the love of life…" is what this moment is about.**

Where did the Tree of Love come from? Here's the answer.

## FROM ONE SEED

From one seed, a mighty tree grows.
From its root, a thousand branches grow.
From its branches, a thousand seeds grow.
From a thousand seeds grows a forest.
From that forest comes a deep reverence for life, all life.

Even the mightiest of trees requires the earth, sun and water.
Even the mightiest of trees requires the darkness of night to rest and brightness of day to grow.
Even the mightiest of trees needs the birds to lite upon its branches.
Even the mightiest of trees needs the smallest creatures of the kingdom to help it grow.
Even the mightiest of trees needs the wind to caress its soul.

From the beginning of time, it has been so.
Even the mightiest needs all things great and small, big and tall, seen and unseen to survive and thrive.
From the beginning of time, we plant the seeds of our children's tomorrows, today.
From the beginning of time, to honor our earth, is to honor ourselves.
Honor your universe. Honor yourself.
Plant the seeds of love, today.

(From this poem sprang the seeds of the Tree of Love chain letter in this book. Go back to page 19 and take a peak to see how you can share the love today.)

# Point to ponder today

> "Each moment of life is as sacred as
> that which goes before it and
> that which comes after it."

# Finding a source of love

An incredible children's book every adult should read at least once in their life is *I'll Love You Forever* by Robert Munch. Read a copy today.

# Classic erotic grape treat

Peel off the outer skin of the grape before eating. This removes a source of bitterness. The grapes taste so sweet! Great if you're alone. Share them with your partner and listen to that mmmmmm.
(Seedless grapes are even less bitter.)

# Why is it...

> When I was a kid, I wanted to grow up.
> Now I am a grown up and I want to be a kid.

Nothing is stopping you from being a kid and seeing the world through child-like eyes, except yourself.

# Be a kid again

On a rainy day, go puddle jumping.

Remember to wear an old pair of shoes, or rubbers.
Do I sound like someone you know?

# Candle light for one is a great way to be in the moment.

Throw in a dash of your favorite music, a pinch of incense and darken the lights. Now breath in slowly and savor the ambiance. Alone, time stands still. Shared with a friend, time flies by.

> *There is only one moment*
> *and that is*
> *NOW*
> *Live it.*
> *Be It.*

# Music to put you in the mood, for living in the moment

Canto Gregorian Chants by Benedictine Monks, EMI Records – you can order it through your local record store.

Temba African Tapestries by Hennie Bekker – to order call The Nature Loft at (905) 773-6848 ask for their catalog. Hennie's music is incredible.

*PS. I am not related to Hennie or the Benedictine Monks.*

# Thought to ponder

"You are a spiritual being.
The human experience is the garden of your soul."

# Sensual point to ponder

"Humor is an aphrodisiac for making love with life."

# Humorous – potentially sensual – point to ponder

Financial success can be accomplished with
25% planning, 25% timing, 25% working, 25% waiting
— or by marrying someone who is already wealthy."

Author Unknown

Feel a little better – that's the proof.

# Enrich your life

Say *'Thank You'* with meaning.

# Why is it...

When I was a kid,
the policeman was someone you trusted and respected,
Now, whenever I get a ticket, I don't trust their judgment.

# Thought provoking saying for today

"To do easily what is difficult for others is the mark of talent.
To do what is impossible for talent is the mark of genius."

Henri Frederic Amiel

# Rediscover spontaneity

The next time it is gently raining, be a kid again and run into the rain. If you really want to enjoy it, don't put on a raincoat, or like a kid, all your clothes.

(Not recommended during thunder and lightening storms.)

# More spontaneity

Have the rain do double duty.
Wear some old clothes. It's okay if they are dirty.
Put a towel in a dry place nearby.
Squirt shampoo into your hair, before getting wet.
Now, make a mad dash into the rain and get wet!
Lather in the soap into your hair and all over your clothes.
Let the rain rinse you and your clothes.

Ahhh! Didn't that feel good.

This can be a lot of fun with a partner. One problem — the soap may not taste too good if you get carried away.

# Rekindling the child within

Share the puddle jumping with your kids or a consenting adult. It is a great way to reconnect to your inner child.

# Point to ponder, for a new day

**"FATE IS WHAT YOU MAKE OF IT."**

# Speaking to the stars — a wishful insight for tonight

Tonight, share this with the heavens above.

"Stars bright, stars light.
The first stars I see tonight.
Wishes were. Wishes might.
May all my wishes come true this night"

Who says you can only have one wish on a starry night. My wish list is extensive and has become a list of dreams turned into realities. Your wish list can come true too. It has to start somewhere and Simon says, "Start it now."

# Point to ponder today, or tonight

"If our reach does not exceed our grasp,
then why is there a heaven."

Robert Browning

# Thought for today

Self-awareness can mean connecting to your inner child. This helps release you from many of the ties that bind you. Reflect on your actions today. Did you blame someone? Did you say I want more and I want it now! Did you needlessly yell to be heard?

Where did you learn these tactics for survival? The difference between surviving and thriving, is learning to take self-responsibility.

Once I realized that the screams and yells of my past were being echoed in the present, in my mind, then I was able to deal with what my childhood had wrought. Then I understood the source of many adult actions.

Learning to become self-aware of destructive emotions, when having them, is very helpful. This is a most liberating insight.

E nrich your life

**CALL UP AN OLD FRIEND.**

P oint to ponder today

"Life is a celebration. Love Living. Live Loving."

W hy is it...

When I was a kid,
I said I'd never be like my parents.
Now I have kids, and I'm like my parents.

R epetition is the staff of life

"The acorn does not fall far from the tree
— now ain't that the truth."

Author Unknown

D iscover a side of yourself that you may not have known exists

In the comfort of your own home, try one of Dick Stupen's Past-Life Regression Ultra Depth Hypnosis CD's or tapes. They really work. To order a catalog or find out where and when he will be doing a seminar call Valley of the Sun toll free at (800) 225-4717. Overseas fax your request to (541) 488-7870.

Trained past-life regression professionals exist in the USA, Canada, UK, Australia and New Zealand. If you are unsure, consult with one. Find them through your local psychiatric or psychological association.

> *When you feel bored, remember that feeling was yours by choice*
> *– consciously or*
> *– subconsciously*
> *Boredom is not a state of the world*

**H**umorous insight for today

"God put me on this earth to do a certain number of things. Now I'm so far behind I will never die."

Author Unknown.

Maybe it is time you reconsidered your priorities.

**E**nrich your life

**BE PATIENT**

**W**hy is it...

When I was a kid, doing my shoelaces up took seconds
Now that I'm grown up,
I'm lucky enough to see my shoes,
forget about tying up the laces.
(Now I understand why they invented loafers.)

**P**oint to ponder today

> "Define yourself not by what you are against,
> but by what you are for."

**P**oint to ponder tomorrow — You're getting ahead of your-self now. Slow down. Savor this moment.

"When you get into a tight place and everything goes against you... never give up then, for that is just the place and time that the tide will turn."

Harriet Beecher Stowe

**E**nrich your life

**Forgive a mistake**

**W**hen you meet someone new, and they say,

> "It's nice to meet you."
> Answer with the following,
> "It's nice to meet someone who
> is such a great judge of character."

**P**onder this

> "To label me, is to invalidate me."

Frederick Nietzsche

# Share the wealth

Take a penny and drop it on the ground. Now the fun begins. Position yourself so that you can see the expression on the face of the person who finds it. Most often, it is cheap entertainment that puts a smile on most folks faces.

Try this in the financial district or by your bank. It's amazing the levels people stoop to spread a little happiness.

P.S. Kind of reminds you of what it is like to be a kid.

# Point to ponder today

"There is no man so blind as the one who claims
it is what you see that counts."

# Upon meeting someone who asks, "How are you doing?"

You say, "Any way I can."

P.S. Not "Anyone I can." Take the opportunity to express and reinforce your desire to accept self-responsibility.

# Nurture tranquility and serenity in your daily life

Self-pity seduces one into an never ending spiral of dissatisfaction with life. Try this to deal with it.

Have a self-pity session with yourself. Set a timer for 6 minutes to be lonely. Then 18 minutes to feel sorry for yourself. When the bell goes off, go for a walk, take a shower, cook, swim and think about something different.

The late actress Joan Blondell used a similar technique. It puts closure on the negative, refocusing you on the positive pleasures of life.

You meet a friend and they ask you, "How are things going?"

Surprise them and just say, "Great!" or "Waking up this morning was enough for me. The rest of the day is a bonus!"

You'll be amazed at their reactions. I've actually seen people change their attitudes over a few months by being responded to in this way.

Point to ponder

"The significant problems we have cannot be solved at the same level of thinking we were at when we created them."

Albert Einstein

When you meet a friend who has lost weight say

"IT'S NICE TO SEE LESS OF YOU."

Watch how they react!

Trivia of the most important kind

A recently conducted survey, in shopping malls across America, found these were the favorite pet names used my men for their women:

| | | |
|---|---|---|
| Sweet Cheeks | Honey | Honey Bear |
| Sweetie | Sweatpea | Snookums |
| Snuggle Bunch | Lover | Babe |

These are the nicknames women used for their men:

| | | |
|---|---|---|
| Honey | Pooky | Honey Bear |
| Babe | Pumpkin | Sugar |
| Honey Bunch | Darling | Dude |

51

# An "Ah–Ha!" story…

## THE MONKS AND THE RIVER BANK

Two Monks were walking in silence along the rivers edge as had been their habit since entering the monastery twenty years earlier. They had both taken a vow to never touch a women and a vow of silence, which neither had broken

They came upon a woman weeping, holding a child in her arms. She noticed them and started to plead, "Dear Monks, please help me cross the river. My child is deathly ill and must see the doctor in the village on the other side of the river. I am too weak and tired to carry him and myself against the rivers tide. Please help me cross the river."

One Monk spoke for the first time in twenty years. "I will help you," he said, gathering mother and child into his arms. He waded across the river, safely deposited mother and child on the river bank, then returned.

The Monks continued on their silent journey along the river's bank.

Many hours later, the other Monk upset by what his companion had done, spoke for the first time in twenty years. He said, "How could you break your vow to never touch a woman and your vow of silence. Look what you have done!"

His friend paused a moment and then replied, "I just carried her across the river. It took me only a few minutes of my time. You have carried her for so much longer."

Enrich your life

**STOP AN ARGUMENT.**

# Try this

"Celebrate each others uniqueness."

# Trivia of the most important kind

The amount of closeness men and women desire in their sexual relationships is not really so different. Men and women share in common six points on a list of ten sexual motives. They both seek intimacy, expression of love, mutual emotional feelings, marriage, the desire to feel loved and the desire to feel needed.

> A study by Elizabeth Allgeier
> Bowling Green State University

> *When it is only a thought, you have the power to assess it and change it if necessary to make it right before giving it life through voice or action*

# The 9 1/2 Laws of Stupidity

Law of stupidity #2.
    The only stupid question, is the one not asked…
        Get what I mean?

    Law of Stupidity # 2.1    "Ah…?"

# Why is it…

When I was a kid,
it was a special treat to go visit grandma and grandpa,
on my way home from school.

Now, if the kids want to visit grandma or grandpa,
they have to make reservations
— for the plane or the train.

# Point to ponder today

"That which does not kill me, makes me stronger."
Frederick Nietzsche

# Trivia of the most important kind

"Young women and older men have similar emotional motivation for having sexual intercourse, while older women and younger men are more physically motivated. The stereotypical pattern reverses in men, as it does in women. Men's physical motivation decreases after age forty, while the love motivation starts rising around age thirty five."
Studies by Joey Sprague, University of Kansas, and
David Quandango, Florida State University

# Take a chance today

"You cannot grow without taking risks. You cannot know people without loving them, which brings its attendant risks of loss and pain."
Eva Figs

# The 9 1/2 Laws of Stupidity

Law of Stupidity # 3.
Stupid is as stupid does. Make stupid mistakes repeatedly until you're ready to get it right.

TIP: Learn from your mistakes – and learn from those of others – you don't have time to make them all yourself.

# Enrich your life

## WARM A HEART

# Why is it...

When I was a kid,
I never wanted to sleep yet always slept well.
Now that I'm grown up,
I always feel tired and rarely sleep well.

Melatonin is a hormone naturally secreted from the pineal gland in the brain. As we age, our body produces less of it. By age forty, the decrease is quite significant.

Melatonin has many properties that can enhance your life according to Dr. Russell Reiter. He is the leading edge researcher on Melatonin. His book *Melatonin: Your Body's Natural Wonder Drug,* is well worth reading. The book won't put you to sleep, but in my experience, Melatonin has helped me sleep better.

Even though it is illegal to sell melatonin in Canada, it is legal to import a three month supply for personal use into Canada. There are numerous mail order companies who will supply you, or come on down for a visit to the USA and pick up a supply for yourself.

# Point to ponder

"If you look like your passport photo,
in all probability you need the journey."

E. Wilson

Incredible and unique holidays are available through Power Place Tours of Laguna Beach, California. Would you like to meet the Dalai Lama, tour the pyramids with the world's leading researchers on them, visit ancient Mayan ruins, explore the power of near-death experiences and much more? Then call to get their catalog, you'll be happy you did.

In the U.S.A. and Canada call toll free 800-234-8687. From overseas call 714-497-5138. Tell them Ken Vegotsky sent you.

Enrich your life

**LOOK FOR TRUTH**

The 9 1/2 Laws of Stupidity

Law of Stupidity # 8.3          Age is an illusion.

> *What I don't use, I may lose. So I stay active for the body think and dream to exercise the mind, and seek spiritually to discover the power of the soul*

When I turned forty, I finally realized my Mom can't be thirty-nine years old anymore. But, the pace of scientific innovation may even change that cherished idea.

(Yes, the numbers aren't in the right order. That's one reason they are called the laws of stupidity — who cares anyhow.)

Get a copy of that old song *I Am My Own Grandpa*

Better yet, make it a mind expanding experience and figure out for yourself how this is possible. It really is!

# Why is it…

When I was a kid, I went to the gym to play.
Now I call it the 'Grunt and Grown' center
'cause that's what I do there.

# Be a kid again

Here's the story of a master at it.

Alan, was five when he taught the family how to imitate Elephant Ears and Girraaafffeeee Necks. We were sitting around the supper table, when the fun just began.

I called my Mom long distance and asked Alan to show her his Elephant Ears.

"No way, Dad," he said. "Grandma can't see me on the phone." For a five year old, he's pretty sharp.

"Alan, try it and ask Grandma if she sees your elephant ears," I said, holding the phone up for him to do his thing. He couldn't resist and put on a great display of elephant ears.

> *Get a charge out of life in more ways than one. Make a long distance call to a loved one today!*

The silence was suddenly broken by his Grandma's voice, "My what wonderful elephant ears you do, Alan. Can I see some more."

A surprised look covered Alan's face. Encouraged he next did his giiirrraaafffeeee neeecckkkk.

Grandma lives a few hundred miles away, but has the sight of an eagle, because she complimented him again – this time about his giiirrrraaafffeeee neeecckk.

This went on for twenty minutes, with his sister, Stephanie, getting into the spirit of things. Between the two of them they created a menagerie of animals and a lot of good cheer. It was well worth the long distance charges.

The nice part is that we did not have to clean up after these household pets.

U se your imagination to enrich your life

Go to the mirror and practice making animal faces.
Then spread a little happiness... practice on some friends.

W hy is it...

When I was a kid and went to the doctor,
he was called family doctor or eye doctor.
As I get older his name has changed
to internist, immunologist, proctologist...
I better end there...

> *Practice makes permanent!*
> *So, practice the right stuff.*

P oint to ponder

"This one step –
choosing a goal and sticking to it –
changes everything."

Scott Reed

T he quick VALUE system for active listening

**V**alidate what the person is saying
**A**ttend to what is being said
**L**isten carefully to the speaker
**U**nderstand what is being shared
**E**mpathize with the speaker

If the speaker is discussing a problem, you may want to take it a step further which is imposing your agenda on them. First ask the speaker if they are interested in changing the situation. If the answer is yes, then ask them what they would like the outcome to be. Sometimes people just want to be heard, and will arrive at a solution once they are ready.

Please note… not everyone is interested in the immediate resolution to their problems. They just want to be heard and acknowledged.

E nrich your life

> Listen actively to what someone is saying.

A n "Ah–Ha!" story…

---

## YEAH, FOR THE HOME TEAM!

I t was 12:26 a.m. when the phone rang out. The ring pierced the peaceful calm of the quiet night. Laini's sister was on the line. Her husband, the successful middle age lawyer, had decided to take his 1962 convertible toy, almost antique car, out for a celebratory drive. The home team had won!!!

What better a time to drive a convertible, especially since the frost only shows in the early morning hours and it was not quite winter yet.

"No, it's too late," Laini answered. She hung up the phone and told me about her brother-in-law's idea.

It does not take much to get me going. So, I started to gently prodded her, "You know, it's a once in a lifetime opportunity. Give it a shot. What do you have to lose?" I must say my gentle prodding was effective. It sold her on the idea before I even had a chance to finish the pitch.

Within minutes Laini was dressed and ready. My wonderful daughter of eight, also dressed and ready, miraculously appeared beside her mom.

"That sure was some pitch I delivered," I noted as I bent over looking to see if Alan, my five year old pride and joy had managed to somehow sneak in there. By this time, I also wanted to get dressed and go. "Where's Alan?" I asked, hopefully.

"Sleeping," came the reply. "Got to go, it's GIRLS NIGHT OUT," Laini said, as the two of them, bundled up in winter clothes, started to get into the 1962 convertible car, otherwise known as Memories.

"Take care," I said, my bathrobe flapping in the cold wind as I leaned into the car. "Watch out. By the way, I hope your insurance is all paid up. I want to sleep comfortably."

As the moans from the convertible's occupants and the sound of the engine were born away on the early winter wind, I stopped for a moment and looked to the stars. I felt how good it feels to be alive.

E nrich your life

**LOWER** YOUR voice

W hy is it...

When I was a kid, fast food meant waiting forever for the TV dinner in an aluminum pan to heat up in the oven.

Now I am grown up, fast food means driving forever to get to a place that takes only minutes to serve my order and sometimes even less for me to eat it!

T he 9 1/2 Laws of Stupidity

Law of Stupidity #5.

If your team is losing, cheer for the other side
...sometimes it is safer that way,
...and sometimes it's more fun.

# Ponder this

**"Embrace life and life will embrace you."**

# Spread a little happiness

The art of throwing smiles is one I've practiced a lot. I look into the eyes of the seminar participants. Then I slowly start to wind up my arm like a pitcher getting ready to toss a ball. As I begin my smile pitching release, I say, "Only the unhappy faces don't smile." You'd be amazed how many catch a smile.

Look someone in the eye and tell them you're throwing a smile onto their face. Then pitch them one.

# Thought for today

"The positive mind has extra problem-solving power."
                                              Author Unknown

# Take an adult consciousness raising course.

There are public seminar centers throughout the USA and Canada where you can meet some of the greatest educators and writers of our time. Here is a partial list of such groups. Look the numbers up in your phone book or check out your local health food store since many carry a free course catalog:

*The Learning Annex:* San Diego, CA; Los Angeles, CA; San Francisco, CA; New York, NY; Washington, D.C.; Toronto ON, Canada
*The Learning Connection:* Providence, RI
*The Learning Exchange:* Sacramento, CA; Wethersfield, CT
*Learning Tree University:* Chatworth, CA

***Leisure Learning Unlimited:*** Houston, TX
***Oasis:*** Chicago, IL
***Discover U:*** Seattle, WA
***Colorado Free U:*** Denver, CO
***Open University:*** Minneapolis, MN
***Knowledge Shop:*** Orlando, FL
***Baywinds:*** Tampa, FL

This is a partial list. Some have been around for years. They are springing up all over the place. Write to the publisher if there is one not mentioned here you feel worthy of noting. The publishers address is at the back of this book.

If you take a course I'm giving, feel free to come up and share an Hawaiian Hug with me. They are great!

# Point to ponder

> "Nothing is so fatal to a partnership
> as not understanding the other."
>
> Walter Dickers

# Today when you eat your meals, practice thankfulness. Say a blessing to the life that gave of itself for your well being.

# Ponder this

**I used to come from the world of seeing is believing.
Now I accept the fact that believing is seeing.**

Knowing that there is a mind-body-soul connection has freed me of many of the anchors in my life. Asked what this connection is, I share the following analogy.

The mind and body are like a magnet. One end is positive, the other end is negative. The magnetic field is what holds the two ends of a magnet together. The soul is the magnetic field for the mind and body. There is a powerful glue that holds everything in place as one cohesive unit. I call it love.

Creativity — one of the most powerful and healing ways

A starter technique to help release your higher creative powers, is called morning pages. This is my simplified starter version.

1. Put a pen and paper by your night table.
2. First thing when you get up in the morning, write down whatever comes into your head. If you cannot think of anything, write 'I cannot think of anything' until you fill up one page. Don't let the inner censor stop you from writing whatever you want. There is no right or wrong content. Think of it as exercising and stretching your creativity muscle. It is not a diary, but a way of tuning into your thoughts.
3. Fill up one page for a start. Then work your way up to three pages a day.

A great book to help you understand and discover your higher creative self is the *The Artists Way* by Julia Cameron, published by The Putnam Berkeley Group. Available in bookstores or order toll free call (800) 788-6262

Action for the day

A little kindness can change the course of one persons life. Given freely, kindness repays itself immeasurably – in more ways than can be known.

The next time you see someone in need, practice thankfulness. Let go of material wants and discover how a little kindness can grow into the abundance of love on this planet called earth.

Turn off that radio station in your head, called W.I.I.F.M. (What's In It For Me). This tidbit is courtesy of professional speaker Paul Litwack.

# Enrich your life

## INSPIRE SOMEONE

# Take a holiday from the usual

Try one of these unique personal development centers. These three have been around for a long time. Call to get their catalogs. What they offer are uniquely refreshing courses and locations.

Esalen Institute, Big Sur, California (408) 667-3000
Omega Institute, Rhinebeck, New York (800) 862-8890
Lily Dale, Lily Dale, New York (716) 595-8721

Write the publisher if you are aware of other Humanistic Development Groups you want considered for inclusion in the next edition, *222 More Ways to Make Love With Life* in the The Love Living and Live Loving™ series.

# Trivia of the most important kind

Aromatherapy uses the essential oils that are distilled from a whole plant or a specific part of a plant. An essential oil can contain as many as 200 organic chemicals and the combination determines the essential oil's properties.

Different essential oil's affect different aspects of the body. For example, essential oil of grapefruit is thought to help suppress appetite and stimulate the immune system. Essential oil of Clary-Sage helps alleviate menstrual difficulties and pain. Tea Tree oil appears to stimulate the immune system and fight viral infections, such as warts. I have used it with my Oral-B electric toothbrush to fight gingivitis gum disease in its early stages. The combination worked so well for me that my gums are rejuvenated. Eucalyptus oil helps me with my respiratory difficulties. When I have a cold or flu, I use it with a facial steamer. I have asthma and have lost the use of one lung due to an accident. Orange oil helps me sleep better at night. I put a drop on my pillow, just below my nose. If it gets on my skin, I find it irritating. These are just a few of the benefits I have discovered about essential oils.

I buy only natural essential oils, preferring them over the synthetic or diluted varieties that some sell as pure essential oils. Two brands I favor are:

– Aromaforce™ by Bioforce, a division of A. Vogel, one of the worlds oldest and leading producers of natural alternative products. Consumer information line call toll free (800) 645-9135. Note: Bioforce U.S.A. Inc. only distributes their herbal, homeopathic, tinctures and body care products in the USA. Their Aromaforce essential oils are only available in Canada.

– Aura Cacia from Frontier Co-operative Herbs. For information or to place orders, call their Herb & Spice Collection line toll free at (800) 786-1388.

Both product lines can be found in better health food stores.

# Enrich your life

## Take a moment of silence

# Why is it...

When I was a kid, a tidy room meant no clothes could be seen, except in the cupboard (Okay, or under the bed)

Now I am grown up, a tidy room for the kids means I can see some empty spots on the floor.

# Enrich your life

## ERASE WORRY

# The 9 1/2 Laws of Stupidity

Law of Stupidity #4.
>When something needs getting done, who do you hire?
>Hire yourself and don't give up.

>*P.S. Remember to fire yourself at the appropriate time.*

# Thought for today

>"Peak performers concentrate on solving problems
>rather than placing blame for them."
>
>Charles Garfield

# Nurture tranquility and serenity in your daily life

Take time for yourself each day by temporarily removing yourself from the daily cares and concerns by:
- Spending a few hours in a botanical garden
- Taking a walk in a park or along a nature trail
- Living a weekend at a spiritual retreat resort

# Memorize this wonderful prayer and repeat it to yourself daily and whenever you are stressed

"God give us the grace to accept with serenity the things that cannot be changed, courage to change the things which should be changed, and the wisdom to distinguish one from the other."

Reinhold Niebuhr created this poem in 1928. He was a professor at New York's Union Theological Seminary.

I have a copy of this taped to my mirror and office wall. It washes away my trials and tribulations whenever I need a quick fix. Reading it, or even better, reading it out loud enables me to connect to the moment so I can better *Make Love With Life*.

# Be a kid for a moment

Climb a tree or Jungle Gym at a park.

# Share the energy

Next time you are with a group of friends, sit in a circle. Have everyone turn so that everyone is facing the back of the person on their left. Now the fun begins. Massage each other's necks and backs. Focus on the caring that is uniting all of you. After a few minutes, turn around and massage the person who was massaging you. Continue doing this as long as you want.

# Why is it...

When I was a kid, my allowance lasted a week.
Now I am older, the money is gone before I even get it?

# Ponder this

"The only thing that should ever be a limitation
is your own dream."

General Colin Powell

# Dream on

One of America's great speakers, Les Brown, says:

**"LIVE YOUR DREAMS."**

# The 9 1/2 Laws of Stupidity

Law of Stupidity #7
Stupid people laugh at themselves.
Really stupid people are the smartest of all,
they laugh even harder at themselves.

Law of Stupidity #7.1
NO is the best shortcut to a yes.
You've just got to remember to accept it and
get on with life.

# Enrich your life

Hug a tree, or
sit down, lean against the tree and daydream awhile.

# Why is it...

When I was a kid, a heavenly body meant hormonal activity, usually in my mind.

Now I am grown up, a heavenly body usually refers to things in the sky or the fact I am hedging my bets with the Heavenly Body on high.

# Take an inspirational time out to say

The Daily Prayer

Grant me the strength to do the tasks that every hour demands.
Give me hope and faith, a happy heart and willing hands.
Be Thou close to me, O Lord, and hear me when I call.
Light a star above my path when twilight shadows fall.
Help me to accept whatever comes my way.
And if I should meet with trials and troubles, this I pray...
Lead me by quiet waters of tranquility
– where my soul may find its comfort and its peace in Thee.

                                              Patience Strong

# Point to ponder today

"There is more power in the open hand
than in the clenched fist."

                                              Herbert Casson

# The 9 1/2 Laws of Stupidity

Law of Stupidity #6

Giving people what they want,
is easier than getting them to
want what you have to give.

# Enrich your life

Visit an old person

# Huggers Heaven

Planet Books offers Hug Coupons, Hug Licenses, Hug Buttons, Hug Kits and a book *Let's Hug: A Manual for Huggers,* edited by Josileen Wilson, all in one convenient location. Get your hugging supplies by writing to Once Upon A Planet, Box 220, Bayside, New York 11361

Sorry, but you won't find my creation, the Hawaiian Hug in her book.

# Simplicity redefined

"The greatest thing a man can do in this world
is to make the most possible
out of the stuff that has been given him.
**This is success,**
and there is no other."

Orison Swett Marden

# Inspirational thought for today

"I have a dream that one day this nation will rise up,
live out the true meaning of its creed:
we hold these truths to be self-evident,
that all men are created equal."

Martin Luther King

# The 9 1/2 Laws of Stupidity

Law of Stupidity #8.
   If your memory is a problem, that's okay –
   make up your own laws of stupidity.
   No ones going to know the difference anyhow!

# Improve your memory

To help your brain function better, try using soya lecithin granules sprinkled on a salad. It has an essential fatty acid, that helps the body and brain function better.

# Trivia of the most important kind

Essential means that your body does not produce the nutrient, which it needs for optimal functioning. Interestingly, modern farming methods deplete the soil of factors critical for the functioning of the human body. Organic farming does not use substitutes to do what nature does best.

# Thought for the day

"Nature is the medicine cabinet for life."

# Cheap first aid for your home

The Aloe Vera plant has medicinal and therapeutic properties. Cuts, burns and other assorted wounds heal quicker when treated with the juice of the Aloe Vera plant. Some people use the juice to help their gastrointestinal tract – stomach and bowels.

Aloe Vera is very easy to use. You just snap off a section of leaf and squeeze the juice onto the problem area.

Easy to maintain, Aloe Vera only requires occasional watering, a little sunshine and a dash of tender loving care to last a life-time.

SELF Magazine is full of life renewing and affirming articles. Each issue has a theme that can enhance your well being. I just discovered a recent issue with an article about Aloe Vera and was very impressed. They have created a magazine that makes a difference in peoples lives. Pick up a copy at newsstands across the U.S.A. and Canada. To subscribe to SELF Magazine toll free call (800) 274-6111.

*P.S. Guys... it is a magazine targeted to women. If you have trouble buying something that isn't macho, buy your favorite lady a subscription and then borrow it.*

# Point to ponder

"The man that makes the greatest mistake
is one who hesitates to attempt changes
for fear of making a mistake."

Lumir Victor Mika

# Discover a whole new world of communications

Visit your local Toastmasters Club. Guests are usually admitted for free and the meetings are fun.

Toastmasters International is a non-profit organization dedicated to empowering individuals using public speaking. The group has over 200,000 members worldwide, and is open to all men and women wishing to improve their general communication skills. It is a grass roots community based group, run mainly by volunteers, and usually very inexpensive to join, if you decide to.

Look in the phone book or call information to find the club closest to you. The world wide headquarters for Toastmasters International is located in Rancho Santa Margarita, California Telephone (714) 858-8255.

# No Toastmasters Club in your area

Then start one. Call the worldwide headquarters for Toastmasters and ask for their help. They will probably give you a contact at a nearby club and suggest they mentor your group.

Many corporations sponsor in house Toastmasters Clubs, since it benefits the staff by helping them to learn how to communicate more effectively. Fact is, it can enhance your life in many ways.

# The 9 1/2 Laws of Stupidity

Law of Stupidity # 9
   Nature has great healing power.
   To get back to nature take a long walk off a short peer
   – just remember to put on your life preserver first!

# Connect to the power within

"Peace comes within the souls of men when they realize their oneness with the universe – when they realize it is everywhere. It is within each one of us."

Black Elk, Lakota Indian Chief

# Enrich your life

Take a walk in a park or nature preserve. Stop and close your eyes. Listen to the symphony of life around you.

# Point to ponder

"When I stopped seeking solitude, it found me."

# Look for natural processes

For example, how old are modern farming methods that use high amounts of manufactured fertilizers?

At the end of World War 2, vast amounts of chemicals used for production in weapons, were left over. The chemical businesses looked for secondary markets. They found their home for these chemicals in the farmlands of America. Thus was born the fertilizer businesses of today.

For fruits and vegetables without chemicals, get organic produce. California has rigid standards for organic farming and organically produced products. Check the processed product labels to see if they are certified organic.

Chemically forced growth causes unforeseen consequences. The plants absorb pesticides and chemicals that can produce toxic cocktails – mixtures – that can affect ones health.

Making love with life means allowing the natural processes to occur, as they were meant to.

# The 9 1/2 Laws of Stupidity

Law of Laziness #1    Do it once. Do it right.

This law just seems to fit under this heading. Besides I felt it was important enough for you to know and decided to be a little lazy.

# Thought for the day

> "Luck is what happens when
> preparation meets opportunity."
>
> Elmer Letterman

# Do an uncommon act of kindness.

Help someone in need today. You could:
   Volunteer to work in a soup kitchen.
   Help someone learn to read.
   Visit a home for the aged, with flowers for the folks.

# Trivia of the most important kind

What does Psychology Today have to say about love? The average person falls in love ten times before getting married. Is that why they say practice makes perfect?

# Throughout time humanity expresses its wonder about nature

> "I think I shall never see
> A poem as lovely as a tree."
>
> A. Joyce Kilmer

# Discover a source of strength

"Take the pooh-pooh of your past, let it become fertilizer for your present, so you may build a better tomorrow, today."

# The 9 1/2 Laws of Stupidity

Law of Stupidity 6.6

Spellin' don't matter, if you don't want anybody to under-stood you. neither does con text.

P.S. I trust my computer to check spelling and make sure every word is write.

# Point to ponder today

> "By mutual confidence and mutual aid,
> great deeds are done, and
> great discoveries are made."
>
> Homer

# Poem to ponder — today and the rest of your life

***IF...***

If you can keep your head when all about you
  Are losing theirs and blaming it on you,

If you can trust yourself when all men doubt you
  But make allowances for their doubting too;
If you can wait and not be tired by waiting,
    Or being lied about, don't deal in lies,
    Or being hated, don't give way to hating,
    And yet don't look too good, nor talk too wise:

If you can dream - and not make dreams your master:
If you can think - and not make thoughts your aim:
If you can meet with Triumph and Disaster
    And treat those two impostors just the same.

If you can make one heap of all your winnings
    And risk it on one turn of pitch and toss,
    And lose, and start again at your beginnings
    And never breath a word about your loss.

If you can talk with crowds and keep your virtue,
    Or walk with Kings - nor lose the common touch,
If neither foes nor loving friends can hurt you.
If all men count with you, but none too much;
If you can fill the unforgiving minute
    With sixty seconds' worth of distance run,
    Yours is the Earth and everything that's in it,
    And – which is more – you'll be a Man, my son!

Rudyard Kipling
writer and poet, born in India in 1865, died 1936

Among his numerous works was the Jungle Book
which was popularized in film by Walt Disney.

# Trivia of the most important kind

Heart felt help from nature! Coenzyme Q-10 is found in every cell of the body, with the highest concentration in the heart.

Japan and European countries use this for treating angina and transient ischemia (mini-strokes).

Numerous small studies have looked at Coenzyme Q-10 for treating a wide range of diseases – cardiovascular disease, high blood pressure, AIDS, muscular dystrophy and periodontal disease to name a few.

This enzyme aids in the production of adenosine triphosphate (ATP), the energy carrying molecule that all life depends on.

Points like this are found in Dr. Andrew Weil's Self Healing newsletter and book *Spontaneous Healing*. To order the newsletter, call toll free (800) 523-3296

# Why is it...

When I was younger and went on a blind date,
it meant that I had to be blind to go on the date.
Now that I am older and single again
when I go on a blind date, I hope the date is blind.

# Enrich your life

Plant herbs in a small dirt pot on your window sill. Chives is a wonderful and easy one to start with. Wonderful in salads, sandwich fixings and soups. It also has healing properties.

> TIP: Home herb gardens are becoming so popular that inexpensive herb starter kits are available at Home Depots and Costco/Price Clubs, on a seasonal basis. (No pun intended.)

# The 9 1/2 Laws of Stupidity — The Final Frontier.

Stupidity is a state of mind. Now it is your turn to start your own list of Laws of Stupidity. Denial is an unhealthy state, so admit it – you, I and everyone else make stupid mistakes daily.

Accept that as a natural part of living and life gets much easier. Instead of kicking yourself in the butt, start a list that makes you laugh at your mistakes – and learn from them too!

Do you have any additions you want to make to The 9 1/2 Laws of Stupidity. Feel free to write me, c/o of the publisher whose addresses are at the end of the book. If used, you may get mentioned, but no cash, in the next book called *222 More Ways to Make Love With Life.*

An "AH–HA!" story…

## THE BANKER AND THE BUM

Fame and fortune can be fleeting. John discovered this the hard way. He had lost it all. His life was reduced to being a bum on the street, begging for hand outs.

John staked out a spot by the biggest bank in town. Day in and day out, he managed to panhandled enough loose change to buy a hot meal. If he was lucky, there was room in the homeless shelter. If not, he slept over the subway gratings, warmed by the hot air coming from them.

Every day the president of the bank would pass by John. At first, he looked at him with disdain. After awhile, he did not even see him.

Now you may ask, what was the lesson John was to learn from this? None that I'm aware of since fate is what it is.

According to my sources on high, the reason John was there was to teach the banker compassion – before it was too late.

Acknowledge a higher power

Humanity throughout the ages has acknowledged a higher power, one which I refer to as the universal intelligence. Here the idea is put so well:

> "Poems are made by fools like me,
> But only God can make a tree."
>
> A. Joyce Kilmer

Ponder this

> "Seek to know yourself and accept others."

# Trivia of the most important kind

Do you have a cold starting?

"Reduce the duration and severity of cold symptoms, by taking 500 milligrams of vitamin C four times a day," says Dr. Elliot Dick, Ph.D., chief of the Respiratory Viruses Laboratory at the University of Wisconsin in Madison.

> TIP: Sucking on one 24-milligram zinc-gluconate lozenge every two hours, up to eight a day, can significantly reduce cold symptoms.

# Ponder this

There are an infinity of universes.

"Impossible!" you say.

Think of it this way. If each individual's perceptions are respected, then they, by their very nature, see themselves as the center of their physical universe. Extending that logic one step further means each life be it human, animal or plant exists in a separate universe – part of and apart from the one you and I exist in. If we go a step further and say every creature exists in a distinctly different universe due to their perceptions, one comes to the conclusion that there are as many universes as there are points of view.

The conclusion to this chain of thought is rather astounding – there is no such thing as right or wrong in terms of another person's perceptions.

> P.S. To thrive and survive requires that we honor each others right to exist, in an ecologically and environmentally sound fashion.

# Thought for the day

"Never. Never. Never. Never give up."
Winston Churchill

# L iberating thing you can do

When you met a stranger, start from a position of trust. This way you'll quickly discover whether or not you can trust them. Distrust takes a lot of positive energy and squanders it, souring the energy.

# S lightly ahead of her time

> **"Love is moral even without marriage,**
> **but marriage is immoral without love."**
>
> Ellen Key
> Swedish feminist and writer — 1849–1926.
> excerpt from her collected works,
> *The Morality of Woman and Other Essays.*

# T hought for the rest of your days

### BE EGOLESS.

By not personalizing the criticism others throw at you, you see it for what it is – a learning experience, one that can help you enter a state of continuous conscious self-improvement. Detaching your ego from the objects of your efforts, helps you move from a state of fear to one of freedom.

# T he Law of Surrender

The secret of a stress free life is found in the 'Law of Surrender'. This is not about giving up, but going with the flow. Accepting reality in the way others perceive it, frees you of the need to impose your perception on others. Giving up the need for control is truly liberating.

Many people choose to be like a fish swimming upstream – against the currents. The amount of energy expended is excessive. Better to follow the flow, and guide yourself accordingly. Only then can you use the power of the system and steer yourself in the direction most suitable for you.

In this way, your actions and thoughts can better be focused on your mission in life and those goals which reinforce it. Conserving your energy and being in partnership with the energy around you ends all struggle.

Focus is directed consciousness, which helps you live fully in the moment.

An "AH–HA!" story...

Here's one my Dad taught me, when I was seven years old. It took decades of living before I understood this powerful time management lesson.

## THE SPECIAL

I was seven years old, when my Dad brought me to Wilensky's for the first time. Dad worked in the garment district. Wilensky's catered to the workers in the area.

I climbed up onto the third generation stool by the counter. It's wooden top was well worn by the seats of thousands who'd come before me.

"What's your pleasure?" the counter man asked.

"Two Specials and two cherry cokes," Dad replied.

"Two Specials coming right up," he said, while mixing two glasses of dark reddish brown syrup with spritzes of soda from the fountain.

Until then, I had only know about soft drinks in bottles.

This was a whole new world to my seven year old imagination.

Unceremoniously the glasses were put in front of Dad and me, quickly followed by two Specials, resting on napkins. I discovered that a Special is a bunch of meat slices, cooked inside a flattened steaming bun.

"Dad, could you cut my sandwich, please?" I asked.

"I don't have a knife," he replied. "Ask the man behind the counter."

I noticed a twinkle appeared in my Dad's eyes, as he spoke.

"Mister, could you cut my sandwich please," I asked Mo, the man standing by the grill, pressing on a bunch of Specials.

Mo stopped and stared at me. He brandished his meat cleaver in the air as he looked me right in the eye. A hush fell over the lunchtime crowd of adults.

> *Focus is a directed form of consciousness*

"Son," Mo said. "No, I can't cut your sandwich." He then waved the meat cleaver from one end of the counter, to the next. Finally it came to rest in front of my seven year old eyes. "You see son, if I cut your Special, then I have to cut everyone's Special who asks me to. That means for the rest of my life I'll be cutting Specials, not making them."

Trivia of the most important kind.

The toe has more nerve endings than the other anatomical parts most people associate with lovemaking. Don't take them for granted. They can be the source of great pleasure – in more ways than one!

Enrich your life

Write yourself a love letter, telling yourself about all your good qualities and acts of kindness you have done and want to do.

**E**nrich your life

"Practice forgiveness and thankfulness daily.
They go hand-in-hand making life a more loving experience."

**L**ast point to ponder

*"GO TO THE END,
TO GET BACK TO THE BEGINNING."*

**H**ugs — vitamins for your mind-body-soul connection.

Hugs add quality to your life as well as offer gentle healing.
I see cuddles and hugs as the origin of therapeutic touch.
Your hugging needs may vary from mine. Use my daily hug
chart as a guideline to discover your hug quotient.

<u>Ken's Daily Hug Chart</u>

3 hugs a day for minimal sustenance of self. It leaves
  you thirsty.

6 hugs a day for nurturing. You feel quenched but still
  unsatisfied.

9 hugs a day for regular growth. Feels good.

12+ hugs a day for inner, outer and spiritual growth. It
  stores some away for those occasional hugging lapses.
  Your mind-body-soul will know this.

An excerpt from The Ultimate Power
How To Unlock Your Mind-Body-Soul Potential
Ken Vegotsky, AGES Publications

**S**avor this moment

"You whose day it is, make it beautiful.
Get out your rainbow colors so it will be beautiful."
Nodjra Song

# An "Ah–Ha!" story...

Here's one a close friend Sevi, shared with me.

---

## The Blanket

"...and she befriended the women's cousin," Sevi said.

The story began in Sweden. Doris, an American tourist, befriended Svetlana, a Swedish women who was going to New York City for the first time. Doris invited her to attend a family wedding during her stay in the big apple.

They were like two little school girls as they boarded the plane to America. Over the summer months they had shared many enjoyable adventures together. Now it was time for Doris to return to her job as a teacher. Svetlana had decided that it was time she visited America.

The plane ride was uneventful, except for one story Svetlana shared.

During World War Two, as a child, the Nazis imprisoned her in a slave labor factory. The Nazis' rules were simple – stay healthy enough to work or be killed.

Beside Svetlana slept Brosnia. Lack of food, medicine and over work weakened Brosnia so much she became deathly ill. Chills and fever took their toll. Yet, she continued to work, the threat of death being a strong incentive.

Svetlana, shared her already subsistence rations with Brosnia. Finally, she gave her the small gray blanket she had to keep Brosnia warm. As if by the grace of God, Brosnia's spirits and health rapidly improved. Enough, that the girls survived the war, finally going their separate ways.

"I always wondered what happened to her after the war... Where she went... How she made out..." Svetlana said. "I guess I'll never know."

The story brought a tear to Doris' eyes. Svetlana rarely

spoke of the war. This showed a part of her friend's past she felt saddened to hear. Doris knew that Svetlana's kindness in the horrid slave camp had meant a great deal.

> *Making love with life means discovering how to give unconditionally of oneself.*

The stories of their past made the hours of flying pass swiftly. Kennedy Airport was a bustling center of activity. The wedding they were going to was the next day. Like school girls they had giggled their way through the flight.

The next day Doris and Svetlana, her new friend from Sweden, went to the wedding. With the ceremony over, it was finally time to eat. Svetlana and Doris sat themselves at a table and six others joined them. As the conversation unfolded, Svetlana talked of Sweden and her life in Europe before the war. How the decades had passed so swiftly.

"You know it's funny," one of the guests said. "I remember almost not making it through the war. I became very ill one time and could barely work. This girl I slept beside shared her crumbs with me. Yet what picked up my spirits the most, was her kindness when she gave me her small gray blanket…"

V ery last to ponder

> O Come, O pure deep love,
> Be there, be now
> Be all; worlds dissolve
> into your stainless endless Radiance
> Frail Living leaves burn
> with your brighter than cold stars.
> Make your servant,
> Your breath, your love

Jelaluddin Rumi

# Bonus point to ponder

"May I always give you more than you pay me for.
May you always want to pay me more."

Pheewww! Said. Did. Done.

Ken Vegotsky

Trust has amazing power. Trust in others starts with trust in yourself. There are over *222 Ways to Make Love With Life* in this book. If you need to count them...

— GOOD LUCK!

*Make Love With Life!*
Start now.

About the
Author...

# Ken
# Vegotsky

Ken is a professional speaker, author and entrepreneur
who has given many keynote addresses and seminars in the
U.S.A. and Canada. He has been featured in print, radio and
TV in the U.S.A., Canada, Australia, New Zealand, United
Kingdom and a host of other countries.

"In recognition of being seen as a model of courage and
hope for others, who demonstrates to all of us the nobility of
the human spirit..." begins the Clarke Institute Psychiatric
Foundation nomination of Ken for a *Courage To Come Back
Award*. These awards were originated by the St. Francis Health
Foundation of Pittsburgh, PA.

Ken has served on the boards of NACPAC (affiliate of the
American Chronic Pain Association) and a half-way home for
mentally challenged people in transition. After numerous
inspirational speeches, Ken was encouraged by listeners to tell
his story.

In the prime of his life, Ken Vegotsky, a successful salesman
and entrepreneur, had a bright future. He was financially
secure, happily married and radiantly healthy. But in one
tragic moment, it all changed. As the result of a parasailing
accident, his world became a blur of pain, hospitals, drug
dependency, obesity and depression.

His National Bestseller, ***The Ultimate Power*** shares his capti-
vating first-person account of his near-death experience, gar-
nished with proven keys for unlocking your personal power.

You'll feel embraced by caring and compassion as you share
his moving experience.

Dear Readers of

### *The Ultimate Power*

Thank you for sharing with me the benefits you've found in using it for study groups. Hearing from you about your body's wisdom to heal itself and the power you have found within yourself, is gratifying.

May *The Ultimate Power* continue to help you to unlock your mind body soul potential and unleash your unlimited potential.

Love

Ken Vegotsky

# *What are people saying about Ken's stories and <u>inspiring self-empowerment presentations?</u>*

"As one professional speaker to another, your keynote presentation was incredibly inspirational, entertaining and unforgettable!"

Paul Waller, Seminar Manager, CPI Plastics Institute.

"Your talk on the Mind, Body, Soul connection was an upbeat and enlightening experience for many of us. Your spiritual search, brought about by personal crisis, lends encouragement to those who are undergoing their own challenges. I heard lots of positive comments from our congregation. Well done."

Larry Meister, President, Unity of London

"Ken is an accomplished speaker who makes his audience feel they are special. He offers keys to appreciating the pleasures of life."

Michael Hobart, Lawyer and President,
The McGill Alumni Association

"Ken's uniquely refreshing presentation gave me valuable insights and tools to use at play and work. I discovered how to unleash the Ultimate Power for success. You will too!"

Rich Treibicz, Area Franchisor, Mailboxes Etc.

"Your ideas inspired my students and me all year. Thanks."

Benjamin Shefler, Professor, Seneca College.

# To Write To The Author

Dear Reader, Meeting Planner, or Speakers' Bureau

Both the author and publisher appreciate hearing from you and learning of the benefits and enjoyment you received from this book. We cannot guarantee that every letter written can be answered by the author, but all will be forwarded. To help ensure that your letter is answered, or to arrange a speaking engagement or seminar, please write to the appropriate address below.

Make your convention or meeting a memorable experience. Book Ken Vegotsky as your Keynote Speaker or seminar/workshop facilitator. He is an entertaining educator. A good time is guaranteed for all!

Ken says, "May I always give you more than you pay for. May you always want to pay me more."

That is Ken's philosophy and a fact!

**In the U.S.A.**

Ken Vegotsky
c/o AGES Publications™
8391 Beverly Blvd., #323-ML
Los Angeles, CA 90048
Please enclose a self-addressed, stamped envelop for reply,
and $3.00 to cover costs.

**In Canada**

Ken Vegotsky
c/o AGES Publications™
1054-2 Centre St., #153-ML
Thornhill, Ontario, Canada L4J 8E5.
Please enclose a self-addressed, stamped envelop for reply,
and $4.00 to cover costs.

**If outside the U.S.A. or Canada**

Enclose international postal reply coupon with a
self-addressed envelope and $3.00 U.S. to cover costs.

Contact Coordinator – phone (519) 396-9553 – fax (519) 396-9554

*A Great Gift for the*
*Special People In Your Life!*

# The Ultimate Power
A National Bestseller!

ISBN 1-886508-15-1

### The Way You Look at Life
### — and Death —
### Will Never Be The Same

Take Control of Your Life
Become the Master of Your Destiny
Learn the Secrets of Living on Your Own Terms
Utilize Your Mind-Body-Soul Potential to
Gain Complete Happiness

"Wow – what a great book. If you are ready to turn on your Ultimate Power, read Ken's brilliant and illuminating book."

*Mark Victor Hansen*
*co-author of Chicken Soup for the Soul*
*New York Times #1 Bestseller*

"As a psychologist – and a human being – I recommend The Ultimate Power to people who suffer chronic pain as well as to people who are searching for their authentic voice and a new beginning to life."

*Dr. J. Siegel, Psychologist*

"Ken Vegotsky has written a GREAT book. A heroic book. He is the Victor Frankl of our day. You will want to purchase many copies to give to those you love, those who are discouraged, those who need to rise again from adversity."

*Dottie Walters, President*
*Walters International Speakers Bureau*
*Author of Speak & Grow Rich*

Lessons from a
**Near-Death**
Experience

# THE
# ULTIMATE
# POWER

## HOW-TO UNLOCK YOUR
## MIND-BODY-SOUL POTENTIAL

Ken Vegotsky

# ORDER FORM

## A LIMITED NUMBER OF AUTOGRAPHED COPIES OF
### THE ULTIMATE POWER
## ARE AVAILABLE FOR CREDIT CARD ORDERS.

YES, I want to order the compelling book, *The Ultimate Power: How To Unlock Your Mind-Body-Soul Potential*. Please send me ____copies at $14.95 each (plus $3.50 for the first and $1.00 for each additional copy to cover shipping and handling). I understand that my order may take from four to six weeks for delivery. Please address my order to:

Name _____

Organization _____

Address _____

_____

City/State/Zip _____

My check or money order for $_____is enclosed.

Please make your check or money order payable to, and send it with your order to:

### AGES Publications
### 8391 Beverly Blvd., # 323-ML
### Los Angeles, CA 90049

Charge my __ Visa ___ MasterCard ___ AMEX

Card #_____expiry date_____

Signature_____

### Credit Card Orders Toll Free
### phone: 1 800 263-1991
### fax: 1 800 458-0025

# A Great Gift for the
## Special People In Your Life

*222 Ways To Make Love With Life*

## ORDER FORM

### A LIMITED NUMBER OF AUTOGRAPHED COPIES ARE AVAILABLE FOR CREDIT CARD ORDERS.

YES, I want to order this delightful book. Please send me ____copies at $9.95 each (plus $3.50 for the first and $1.00 for each additional copy to cover shipping and handling). I understand that my order may take from four to six weeks for delivery. Please address my order to:

Name _____

Organization _____

Address _____

_____

City/State/Zip _____

My check or money order for $_____is enclosed.

Please make your check or money order payable to, and send it with your order to:

### AGES Publications
### 8391 Beverly Blvd., # 323-ML
### Los Angeles, CA 90049

Charge my __ Visa ___ MasterCard ___ AMEX

Card #_____expiry date_____

Signature_____

### Credit Card Orders Toll Free
phone: 1 800 263-1991
fax: 1 800 458-0025

## Combined Into One Special Offer

# 222 Ways To Make Love With Life

### and

# The Ultimate Power

## *ORDER FORM*

**YES**, I want to order both books as a set. Please send me
____sets of these book at $24.90 per set. I understand that I will
receive free shipping and that my order may take from four to
six weeks for delivery. Please address my order to:

Name _____

Organization _____

Address _____

_____

City/State/Zip _____

My check or money order for $_____is enclosed.

Please make your check or money order payable to, and
send it with your order to:

AGES Publications
8391 Beverly Blvd., # 323-ML
Los Angeles, CA 90049

Charge my __ Visa ___ MasterCard ___ AMEX

Card #_____expiry date_____

Signature_____

Credit Card Orders Toll Free
phone: 1 800 263-1991
fax: 1 800 458-0025